THE POTENTIAL LEADER

Irene u. Matthias Winkler
Teutonenstraße 86
D - 58509 Lüdenscheid
Tel. Priv. 02351 / 380768
Tel. Gesch. 02351 / 24024

THE POTENTIAL LEADER

DR. COSTA S. DEIR

Cityhill Publishing
Columbia, Missouri

ISBN: 0-939159-12-0

**INTERNATIONAL LEADERSHIP
SEMINARS**
7245 COLLEGE STREET
LIMA, NY 14485 USA
(716) 582-2790
WE WELCOME YOUR ORDERS

INTRODUCTION

*T*his book, a collection of biblical leadership principles, presents compact capsules of wisdom for personal study. The proverbial concepts presented here will help keep the leader's mind awakened to receive truth.

Each statement is brief, focused, and easily understood. Filled with rich variation, these principles strike at times the emotions, at times the intellect. But above all, they move the will toward greater Christian progress.

Like light beams of truth, these principles can, by the force of their illumination, show you brighter, healthier paths of living. Put into practice, they will modify your ways of thinking, choosing, and acting. They will always aim you toward excellence, always move you toward higher and higher levels of maturity in Christ.

1

Walking in the fear of God is the first prerequisite to leadership.

Phil. 2:12

No leader can have a true vision of God's purpose for his life until he knows what is in God's heart; to acquire this knowledge he must walk in the fear of God.

Ps. 25:14

A leader's relationship to God should be the first divine principle of life; it guarantees the success of his leadership.

Prov. 3:5-6

The leader who has an awakened sense of dependence upon God continually makes his relationship with God genuine in his daily experience.

John 15:5

Blessed is the leader who realizes that relationship with God must be sealed with a commitment, the continuing cost of which is submission to the Holy Spirit to work the cross principle in his life. Only as he is willing to pay such a price, continually cooperating with the Holy Spirit, can he expect to strengthen his relationship with God and change from what he is to what he ought to be.

Luke 9:23-24

The quicker a leader responds to God, the quicker he reveals the strength of his commitment in his relationship to God; hesitancy reveals struggling of the will.

John 2:5

*T*he closer a leader lives to God, the more serious he becomes in his relationship, walk, and service to Him.

Ps. 37:23-24

The deeper the leader's relationship with God, the more calm within and quieter without he will be—the deeper the river, the less noise it makes.

Ps. 37:37

9

When a leader's relationship with God is right, he experiences the joy of the Lord within his soul. This joy makes his face radiant, his personality sparkling, and his manner charming.

Ps. 16:11

When a leader is out of right relationship with God, his language and his behavior betray him.

Matt. 12:34-35

The leader who is starved spiritually will not experience the reality of God in his daily life, and he has nothing to offer his followers but empty husks.

Luke 4:4

Unless a leader meets God afresh and comes broken before Him daily, he is of no real use to God and His cause.

Prov. 29:1

The leader who is easily influenced by his environment rather than influencing it reveals inner instability due to lack of maintaining a right relationship with God.

John 10:12

When a leader establishes and maintains a strong relationship with God, it instills in him full assurance in every step he takes and makes him one who dares to do the impossible.

Num. 14:24

A leader who maintains a right relationship with God through daily fellowship proves practically that his experience with the Lord is always fresh and refreshing to others.

Ps. 84:5-7

The life of the leader who lives beyond the veil, meeting with God afresh on a daily basis, is characterized by brokenness, contriteness, emptiness, and a sense of nothingness, yet he enjoys the overflow of God's fullness.

Isa. 57:15

A leader may have a great history of successful accomplishments, but unless he maintains his daily walk with God in a progressively closer relationship he will find himself on the brink of disaster by relying on the past.

Phil. 3:12-14

Just like a poor sheep that cannot carry his own wool, so is a poor leader who cannot carry his own responsibilities; he soon disqualifies himself from the role of leadership, because leadership and responsibility are synonymous.

Prov. 27:23

*T*he leader who neglects his responsibilities, refuses to take personal responsibility for his operation, or does not discipline himself is absolutely unfit to discipline his followers. No leader has a right to make boundaries for his people which he himself refuses to stay within; there are no free-lance leaders in the role of true leadership.

Luke 14:25-27,33

God will never entrust a leader with a greater responsibility to accomplish greater things for His Kingdom if he is unfaithful in doing the little things, considering them to be unworthy of his attention.

Matt. 25:21

*E*ach responsibility that a follower carries out faithfully to its completion is a confirmation that he is a potential leader.

1 Cor. 4:2

An alert and responsible leader does not have to be reminded to perform his duties, for he is always at his best.

Prov. 12:24

An exemplary leader knows the most valuable gift he can give is his godly example for others to follow.

2 Thess. 3:7-9

*T*he example of Christ should be the pattern of life for every leader whose greatest quest is to be a faithful under-shepherd.

1 Pet. 5:1-4

A godly leader knows that being an example is a way of life, not something extra to put on, and he endeavors to live his best for God daily.

Matt. 5:14-16

2

*T*he leader who does not express Christ's life in his daily walk does not have much to offer, even though he may be a most eloquent speaker.

2 Cor. 4:10-11

The role of leadership demands a Christ-like example for others to follow; consequently, the one who is a slave to destructive habits disqualifies himself as a leader.

Rom. 6:12-22

Whenever a leader so values eternity that he invests his life, his time, his talents, his gifts, and his substance into it, he begins to live a life worth following.

2 Pet. 3:10-14

*T*he leader who lives on borrowed talents, borrowed money, and borrowed time has no right to be in leadership and must eventually declare his bankruptcy of character—the sooner the better.

Matt. 25:1-13

The less a leader values time, the bigger fool he becomes; the more he values time, the wiser he becomes. Time is the most valuable thing God offers us in this life to fulfill His will and purpose.

Ps. 90:12

Proper, wise, and divinely inspired planning in the life of a leader enables him to save much time, which he can then invest in fulfilling the will of God.

Prov. 24:3-6

A leader reveals the depth of his consecration to God by the way he handles the money God entrusts to him.

Matt. 25:14-30

*B*ecause they lack self-discipline, some leaders are walking disasters when it comes to handling money.

Luke 16:1

A knowledgeable leader knows God desires that he develop his talents to the best of his ability and that he diligently and systematically strives to reach his full potential, accepting the price of discipline to make it a reality.

1 Tim. 4:15

An excellent leader, with great diligence, develops excellence in the talents, gifts, and abilities that God has given him; a prepared heart and a prepared mind, joined with a prepared will, make for excellence in leadership.

Dan. 5:12

A leader who is unable to handle his wife and children wisely is not fit to handle people outside his own home.

1 Tim. 3:1-5

The greatest testimony of a mature leader comes from his own family.

Ps. 128:1-6

The leader who makes Jesus the center of his marriage will have zest, sparkle, and exuberance continually as Jesus continues to change the water of his daily life into the wine of spiritual living, where the more abundant life is enjoyed.

Eph. 5:2,25

The leader whose philosophy of marriage is to consider it a great privilege to faithfully overwhelm his spouse with a love which flows out of his joyful position in Christ will take the drudgery and coldness out of daily duties. Instead, he will continuously renew the atmosphere of love as he fulfills these duties, and the two will thrive together.

Eph. 5:25-26

A leader who neglects the training of his own children has no future; neither will his children.

Prov. 22:6

A leader's home should be most important to him. Here he should put forth his best efforts to produce in his children the best of God's qualities, not depending on the school to do that, for the school takes what qualities the home produces as a base upon which to build. Then society builds on the foundation which the home, the church, and the school have established.

1 Tim. 3:4-5

The quality and maturity of leadership determines the success or failure of an operation.

Josh. 5:13

Unless there is sufficient evidence of maturity in a candidate, he should not be chosen or considered for the role of leadership. Otherwise it would be detrimental to him and the whole operation.

1 Tim. 3:1-6

A mature leader is governed by divine principles and the Spirit of the Lord, rather than by changing circumstances and the moods of others.

Gal. 5:16

The leader who welcomes the dealings of the Holy Spirit to mature his life will also enjoy the guidance of the Holy Spirit, which will save him from missing the perfect will of God.

Ps. 40:8

The leader who submits to the Lordship of Christ guarantees his own maturity.

Phil. 2:9-11

*H*ow a leader overcomes obstacles on the way toward his accomplishments reveals the level of his maturity and experience.

1 Sam. 17:32

Resiliency is one of the greatest signs of maturity in a leader; it is the greatest saving factor in his life.

Acts 5:40-42

A mature leader accepts the responsibility of his failures rather than denying or justifying them.

Prov. 28:13

An immature leader is basically irresponsible and unaccountable.

Prov. 25:19

3

*E*very wise leader assumes full responsibility for building his own character, and he helps others do likewise.

1 Cor. 3:9-15

The test of a leader's character is not revealed in the exceptional moments when he is at the height of success, but in the ordinary tasks he performs on a daily basis.

Phil. 2:12

The leader who has developed nobility of character motivates rather than manipulates.

1 Sam. 17:36-37

Unless a prospective leader learns how to follow with humility of heart, there is no hope for him to become someone who should be followed.

Matt. 4:19-20

Poor leaders are those who were poor followers.

2 Tim. 4:10

Prospective leaders who refuse to play second fiddle because of their imagined greatness may never be able to play the first, for the best leaders have been the best followers.

Rom. 12:3

Failure to lead and refusal to follow disqualifies a person from a position of leadership. He should at least be honest enough to get out of the way rather than hinder the purposes of God.

1 Sam. 15:23

Before training a potential leader, the greatest signs to look for are tenderness, brokenness, and contriteness. If none of these are found, wait until God takes him through His mill; otherwise you are wasting your time battling a stubborn will and a proud spirit.

Isa. 66:2

When God manages to break a man, He will succeed in making him a great leader—not necessarily great in himself, but great in obedience to His daily commands.

Acts 9:1-9

A broken leader enjoys continual inward transformation as he meets God afresh each day.

Isa. 57:15

The leader who desires to lead others must prefer others.

Phil. 2:3

The leader who thinks God has chosen him because he is so great automatically disqualifies himself.

Prov. 6:16-17

Some leaders have such high opinions of themselves that they disqualify themselves from the role of useful leadership.

Gal. 6:3

An unreasonable leader automatically disqualifies himself from leadership.

1 Kings 12:6-8

A leader who pouts and is unable to accept a difference of opinion disqualifies himself from leadership.

1 Cor. 11:18-19

A serene leader, because of the strength of his relationship with God, never loses his calm, regardless of the turbulence he is going through.

John 16:33

31

The pressures of adversity and of all kinds of added responsibilities come to leaders whose quest is to reach higher goals; only the secure, the stable, and the steadfast can get through these pressures without breaking.

Ps. 27:3

*W*hen a prospective leader moves out of the crowd into the spotlight, everyone is ready to criticize him and judge him; but by his character, intent, and performance, he proves whether or not he has what it takes to lead.

Matt. 7:15-20

Insecurity in a leader, as well as self-doubt and embedded fear, hinder him from being a candidate for leadership.

2 Tim. 1:7

32

The search continues for highly disciplined prospective leaders who prove themselves to be great achievers.

Dan. 11:32

*O*nly the leader who lives the crucified life on a daily basis, just as Paul who declared, "I die daily," becomes most effective in his mission in life.

1 Cor. 15:31

The leader whose supreme purpose is to fulfill his Master's will and to whom the cross is a reality in his daily life, will find no challenge too great, no place too difficult, no task too tiresome, and no field too hard.

1 Cor. 4:9-16

The most outstanding leader is the one who motivates himself to action without outward stimulation.

Phil. 3:13-14

No one will ever become a leader as long as he waits for others to motivate him to action.

Ps. 87:7

Diligence in preparation usually pays the greatest dividends.

2 Tim. 2:15

4

*T*he leader who settles for average with no
ambition to diligently move to excellence is
not fit to be followed.

Phil. 3:7-15

Some leaders are directly called of God and
are taught and disciplined by Him in order
to move them into responsible leadership
positions.

Jer. 1:5

A stable leader takes the place God has assigned to him. Out of his relationship with God, he ministers with confidence, authority, and a most gracious manner to those whom God has given to him to serve.

Acts 27:21-26

A leader who usurps authority plays into the hands of Satan.

1 Pet. 5:3

Some leaders do well socially, economically, financially, and administratively but not spiritually. Such individuals may lead men in the world, but not in the church.

Luke 4:4

Whatever a leader is called upon to bear, he is divinely enabled by the anointing he receives as he daily waits on the Lord to charge his battery afresh.

Isa. 61:1

Many times a leader finds his responsibility overwhelming, but he continues to maintain his spiritual glow as he serves the Lord, knowing that He who has called him continues to divinely enable him; he has learned to draw from the strength of the Lord.

2 Cor. 4:16

Leaders who embrace the operations of the cross on a daily basis enjoy the victory of His resurrection and are endowed with such fresh anointing from the Throne that they excel beyond their peers.

Gal. 6:14

The leader who enjoys a daily supply of the Spirit of the Lord revels in the fresh anointing that excites him and enables him to perform the Word of God for the day.

Acts 4:13-31

When a leader meets God on a daily basis, he will be refreshed with the revelation of God's mind and purpose and endowed with fresh anointing; he will be able to refresh others wherever he goes.

Ps. 84:2

A leader who is devoid of the anointing of the Holy Spirit but who endeavors to perform for God by his own abilities, talents, gifts, and intelligence is an abomination to God.

John 15:5

Preparation today in the life of a leader gives him the ability to fulfill his responsibilities in the tomorrows to come.

Heb. 5:7-8

When a potential leader harbors leadership ambitions before he is properly prepared, he is courting disastrous failures; adequate preparation coupled with rich experience is the key to successful administration.

1 Tim. 3:10

*P*reparation is an extremely important start for every action in life; unprepared leaders are professional failures.

Luke 14:27-33

Failure in any operation is always attribut-able to inadequately prepared leadership.

2 Pet. 1:5-10

*T*he leader who has little time for preparation and less for meditation will lack fulfillment in ministry and will eventually end up in a state of frustration and degradation.

Ps. 1:2

A leader whose talent proves to be raw will have a hard time developing the full talents and abilities of his people.

Acts 18:24-26

A leader who doesn't have anything has nothing to contribute to others.

Prov. 25:14

Continual preparation in the life of a leader guarantees continual success.

Josh. 1:8

An ambitious leader lives a life of continual preparation from one stage to another with his eyes on his ultimate goal, knowing that his effectiveness in every phase of life is dependent on the measure of his preparation.

Phil. 3:12-14

It is absolutely important that a leader in every way utilize his full potential and totally give of himself.

Rom. 12:1-2

A leader must of necessity keep spiritually fit by maintaining his daily walk with God by saturating his mind with the richness of revelations from God's Word while shutting himself in with God in the secret place, enveloped by His sweet presence.

Ps. 27:4

The University of the Holy Spirit is open for applicants on a permanent basis.

John 14:26

It is not the leader who holds high degrees from prestigious, Ivy League institutions that succeeds in the Kingdom of God, but the one who is daily taught the Word of God in the School of the Holy Spirit.

John 14:26

In the University of the Holy Spirit, the only leaders who graduate are the ones who are broken in spirit, who have mellowed and become tender and contrite, who easily respond to His leadings and are willing to submit to His dealings and who find it a delight to obey His commands; such become most trusted and greatly entrusted.

Ps. 51:17

5

*S*upervised training trips for a potential leader
precede performance trips upon maturing.

Acts 12:25

A novice leader has a long way to go before
he can be trusted and entrusted, for he has
to walk a proven path.

1 Tim. 3:6

Life is not easy for the potential leader in training, nor for the trainer, until the rough edges have been filed smooth.

Prov. 27:17

*T*o lead, one must learn to follow; to follow, one must be teachable in attitude, humble in spirit, and receptive to discipline, welcoming needed correction.

2 Chron. 34:27

It behooves prospective leaders to be humble, teachable, and receptive to correction if they are ever to prosper along the way to reaching the height of their calling.

James 4:6-10

The leader who does not grow in humility on a daily basis is not learning the first lesson of leadership.

Isa. 57:15

Before a prospective leader can be taught he must have a teachable and humble spirit, which guarantees him receptivity.

Matt. 23:11-12

The only leader who makes progress is the one who is teachable and receptive to others.

Heb. 13:17

A teachable leader must have two important qualities: 1) eagerness to learn and 2) determination to overcome the obstacles to learning; these supply him with great assurance against discouragement in the learning process.

Prov. 4:13

A novice leader's teachableness is the gateway to his excellence.

Hos. 4:6

A teachable leader learns, by quick observation, from the failures of others rather than waiting to learn from his own, which are more costly.

Prov. 24:32

The receptivity of a novice leader is the doorway to his progress.

Prov. 10:8

If an apprentice leader is ever going to make progress into maturity, one great truth he needs to know well is that while in training he must be open to correction with a humble spirit and an appreciative attitude.

Prov. 28:14

Correction to a leader may be bitter medicine, but it yields the sweetness of Christ when it is accepted, digested, and assimilated. The leader who responds to correction comes into perfect alignment with the will and purpose of God for his life.

Heb. 12:5-11

The leader who accepts correction when needed rather than resenting it will make the quickest progress in his leadership and gain the confidence of his brethren.

Prov. 9:9

The leader who earnestly asks the Lord on a daily basis to deal with his feelings, reasonings, and will and to bring them in tune with Him is sure to make progress in his walk with God.

Isa. 55:8-9

A smart young leader must be smart enough to realize how young and inexperienced he is and begin to open up unreservedly to God and to more mature leaders so he can derive that which is best in God for his life; he will certainly be a winner-at-large.

Heb. 13:17

The wisest among potential leaders is the one who befriends wise and effective leaders and learns from their many years of experience as much as he possibly can and preserves what he learns to share with others.

Prov. 13:20

A prospective leader who has an eager spirit to learn all he can from the rich deposit of those who have proved their role in leadership will be enriched greatly and make strides in the process of his development.

Prov. 23:12

The leaders of the future who are coming up on the horizon, having taken the venturesome step forward, covet fatherly leaders who have gone through the battles of life learning valuable lessons that can be of great importance to them.

1 Cor. 4:14-17

Unless a leader learns everything he possibly can on a daily basis directly from God and indirectly through others, there is no hope for him to make progress in his walk with God, let alone in serving Him.

Prov. 13:10

Until a leader makes progress in self-discipline he does not make progress in anything else in his life or ministry.

1 Cor. 9:24-27

Success in every leadership role, regardless of the level, is not a miracle from outer space as some may suspect, but is due to skill coupled with diligence and self-discipline.

Prov. 11:27

*K*now-how, self-discipline, and whole-hearted diligence on the part of a leader guarantees him success and brings him fulfillment.

Mark 12:29-30

The leader who is systematic in his discipline succeeds, but the leader who is sporadic always fails, for he resorts to his feelings to guide him.

Josh. 1:8

6

*T*he leader who translates his good ideas into habits and then develops them as patterns for his life will climb the ladder without many obstacles along the way.

James 1:22

A novice leader's self-discipline leads him to great accomplishments.

Rom. 6:12-13

A choosy leader who chooses the choicest things must pay the highest price himself.

Matt. 13:44-45

A skillful leader realizes he cannot use someone else's brain but has to develop his own if he desires to excel.

Prov. 24:14

Prospective leaders must pay the price of added self-denial and self-discipline to supplement their training in order to be made what they ought to be.

2 Tim. 2:3-4

Only the leader who is fully convinced that he has not reached his full potential will press on in seeking the Lord, being diligent to continue developing his character and his God-given talents.

Phil. 3:12-15

A leader who exercises self-denial coupled with self-discipline while being directed by the Holy Spirit to fulfill the will of God will be great in God's kingdom, for God trusts much to those of such quality.

1 Cor. 9:24-27

*T*he leader who is willing to pay the greatest price in self-denial and self-discipline will be the first to come to the forefront.

2 Cor. 11:23-28

Every prospective leader should know how to command his actions and how to control his reactions if he is to make progress in the process of his development.

Luke 23:34-46

A prospective leader who accepts discipline delightfully, regardless of his feelings, will grow the fastest and will have a bright future in the role of leadership.

Acts 16:23-25

A submissive leader knows well that Christ does not become his Lord just by his saying, "He is Lord," but by submitting to His revealed will on a daily basis; this submissive leader enjoys his walk with God.

Gen. 6:9

The potential leader whose aim is to obey God in the big things to do great things must of necessity begin to obey God in the little things, which really matter in his training for greatness.

Heb. 10:7

The prospective leader who has a submissive spirit makes the fastest progress in his growth toward what God intends him to be.

Luke 2:51-52

*V*oluntary submission on the part of prospective leaders makes their training a joy to them and to their leaders, and things move smoothly and sweetly.

Heb. 13:17

The potential leader who learns to submit to authority over him will exercise proper authority when his turn comes.

Matt. 8:5-13

The leader who makes gratitude a part of his daily living enjoys life and is never tempted to take God, people, or blessings for granted.

Eph. 5:17-20

*W*hen a leader is grateful to God for the sufferings and the resurrection of Jesus Christ, he dedicates himself wholly and unreservedly and pays the price of self-denial on a daily basis to walk with Him.

2 Cor. 12:1-10

A potential leader can only be helped when he receives the needed help with a grateful heart and an appreciative spirit.

Ps. 141:5

Before a prospective leader can hope to make any strides toward gaining the confidence of others, especially his superiors, he needs to prove himself to be respectful, appreciative of their help, and receptive to their correction.

Eph. 5:20-21

A leader who possesses a grateful heart for the grace of God that lifted him from the miry clay into a place of right relationship to the Father becomes a lifter-at-large.

2 Cor. 1:3-7

A novice leader's respectability leads him to acceptance without the laborious, exhausting task of trying to prove himself in many other ways.

1 Tim. 4:12

A secure leader does not resort to jesting and joking and making light remarks in order to entertain others and find a place in their hearts, for he knows that in doing so he would lose their respect.

Eph. 5:1-4

A respectable leader never disregards the confirmations of others, but seeks them for his safety and for the assurance that it brings to the hearts of those surrounding him.

Matt. 18:15-17

A respectable and ethical leader does not take liberties that do not belong to him.

Gal. 5:13

7

A covetous leader, whether he covets position, prestige, popularity, or money, ruins himself early in life.

Eph. 5:5

A foxy leader is eventually caught by his subtle ways in the same trap he sets for others.

Ps. 57:6

A conniving leader may win for a season until people discover his ways; but when they do, backfiring is heard loud and clear everywhere.

Num. 32:23

*A*n undisciplined leader has no right to lead, for he is not an example of what he intends his followers to be.

Phil. 3:7-21

A leader who neglects self-discipline due to an inflated ego and high position, ends up missing God and creating unlimited messes.

Luke 14:26-27

The leader who cannot trust the Lord for everything will not be able to trust Him for anything.

Heb. 11:6

The leader who, through faith in his living God, attempts to do the impossible beyond his natural abilities will experience the reality of supernatural power in his daily life.

Mark 9:23

When a leader has unrealistic expectations beyond the permission of the Holy Spirit, he ends up in disappointment.

Ps. 19:13

The difference between setting realistic goals and unrealistic ones is in the ability and maturity of the leadership. Inexperienced leaders tend to set higher goals than they have the ability to achieve, and thus become frustrated and discouraged, and quit.

John 19:30

Novice leaders aspire for greatness the cheapest way possible with as many short-cuts as possible, not knowing that those two methods violate the major process of leadership development.

Prov. 28:20

Many a novice leader endeavors to put himself on the same level as those who are more experienced and mature, vying for the same acknowledgment and opportunities, not knowing that bypassing the process and the price to reach that level is a form of subtle deception that many fall into.

Rom. 12:3

Prospective leaders are susceptible to deception due to unguided ambition.

James 3:13-16

*T*he greatest fool is the one who fools himself. No leader can afford to be one.

Gal. 6:3

A leader who is blind to himself cannot lead others without hurting them.

Matt. 15:14

A leader who seeks to please everyone so everyone will speak well of him will not do well in anything, for that is the height of deception.

Luke 6:26

A leader who labors under a false compulsion, a competitive spirit, and a wild zeal has an early appointment with the undertaker.

Num. 16:28-30

A leader who is always disputing for preeminence is competing with the preeminence of Christ.

3 John 9-10

A quest for prominence among novice leaders plagues them continually and makes them competitive in their endeavors to prove themselves efficient.

Num. 12:1-9

When a novice leader rejects correction, he transfers his credentials to the Association of Fools.

Prov. 15:5

The leader who refuses further instruction and correction when needed lives in the height of deception, thinking he has arrived.

Prov. 15:10

*M*any promising prospective leaders would have come to full fruition had they learned to submit to the suggestions, corrections, and counsel of those who are more mature.

2 Tim. 3:16-17

The leader who is choosy about whom he takes correction from stays imperfect.

Prov. 15:10

Prospective leaders discover the measure of their hidden pride when they are given orders to carry through and when they are being corrected. What a discovery!

Matt. 21:28-31

The leader who is afflicted with the "I" disease needs major surgery by the master "I" (eye) surgeon before he can lead others, since he is blind to himself.

Prov. 16:5

It is hard to convince some novice leaders who are coming up the ladder that they are novices and need to learn; evidently they stopped learning when they got their diplomas and forgot that their graduation day was called commencement.

Prov. 15:31-32

8

A leader who continues to have his own way stays a baby. We only grow up as God has His way in our lives; and His ways are perfect.

Prov. 15:32

To a proud potential leader, no one really counts but himself, for he considers himself the first, the last, and everything in between—no wonder he fails his training!

Prov. 16:5

High self-opinion is the poisonous atmosphere that proud potential leaders breathe wherever they go, and yet they wonder why people resent and reject them.

Matt. 23:12

There are no elevators in the kingdom of God to cater to lazy leaders who want to ride them to the heights; the ladder of success awaits those who will diligently persist in taking one step at a time upward toward the goal.

Job 23:11-12

Rebellious leaders are stubborn in will and bitter in attitude; because they are irresponsive, they become irresponsible; they join the Escapists' Club.

1 Sam. 15:17

Blessed is the leader who knows that rebellion is deeply ingrained in his human nature and that stubbornness is in the nucleus of every atom in his being; blessed is the leader who comes to the Lord's clinic for daily cleansing, for he shall be safe from the sweeping demonic epidemic of the anti-Christ spirit.

2 Thess. 1:7-10

The potential leader who rebels against authority over him will exercise a domineering spirit should he come to a place of authority.

1 Pet. 5:1-6

Until a leader stops resenting daily changes in his life and learns to adjust as the need arises, he will never make daily progress.

Ps. 139:23-24

A leader who leads a loving life toward his Lord leads a disciplined life to please his Lord; for love is the only motivating factor that helps us to discipline ourselves without resentment.

John 15:10

When a leader allows his personal feelings to stand in the way of his progress, his feelings become his greatest enemy.

Titus 2:6-8

*E*very leader who wants to enjoy the full privileges of his role must take full responsibility for his faults, his words, and his deeds, because he is fully accountable to God.

Prov. 28:13

Accountable leaders are more careful in their behavior and performance and are safe to follow.

1 Cor. 4:9-16

*N*o leader who shuns accountability can be trusted.

Matt. 25:14-30

One of the major responsibilities a prospective leader has when assuming a responsible position, regardless of its level, is to know the revealed will of God in every decision he makes and to be free and loyal enough to stand by that decision.

Exod. 18:19-22

In order to proceed with purity and clarity of vision, it behooves spiritual leaders to continually seek God daily for a fresh unfolding of His will.

Ps. 86:3

*U*nless a leader is really in tune with God moment by moment, there is no way he can set his priorities to fulfill the will of God on a daily basis.

Ps. 86:11

The leader who continues to miss God's will in making decisions due to his foggy mind and hasty spirit kills the desire of the people to follow him.

Prov. 14:12

The potential leaders who are well informed about their role best perform their responsibilities.

Isa. 28:23-29

*E*ach prospective leader needs to update his information as well as his job description to gain the desired progress.

Prov. 24:4-5

A leader who keeps himself well informed in all areas of his involvement also keeps himself greatly motivated to intelligently perform his best.

Jer. 10:23-24

After a period of training, a prospective leader must be given opportunities to flourish on his own, just like eaglets are given a chance to exercise their wings.

Titus 1:4-5

*M*any a leader cannot perform his daily duties because of a sluggish system that is fighting its own civil war within its ranks.

Prov. 24:30-32

A leader's health can be his best friend only as he daily detoxifies his system and energizes it with nutrition; this will give him the stamina he needs to carry on his responsibilities and enjoy life to the full.

Prov. 30:8

It's God's intention that leaders motivate people to righteousness and wholeness.

Luke 3:7-14

A leader who does not always take the initiative to inspire and motivate his followers disqualifies himself from leadership.

Judg. 7:15

9

A leader in a high position has great leverage in the lives of the people under his jurisdiction; what an awesome responsibility before God and man.

2 Sam. 23:3

It is an awesome responsibility to be a leader because all eyes look to you, expecting idealism, heroism, and perfection.

Phil. 3:17

When a leader neglects to nourish his soul with the Word of the Lord on a daily basis, he becomes spiritually anemic and vulnerable—no wonder his followers starve to death!

Job 23:12

*T*he force of example is the greatest, for it speaks the loudest, compelling others to follow.

Acts 1:1

A leader's godly example exerts a godly influence far beyond the most persuasive words.

Acts 14:19-22

A godly leader, by his example, affects the way people live.

2 Thess. 3:7

Truth becomes more powerful when it is lived out in the life of a leader; such a leader compels others to follow by his godly influence and example.

Luke 9:57

People naturally gravitate to a gentle leader who does not force issues on them but leads by example, showing what he desires his followers to be and to do.

Ps. 18:35

If the presence of a leader does no good to his operation, his absence will do no harm.

Phil. 1:21-26

A leader whose influence does not carry far, especially among his own people, is unfit to continue in his post.

1 Kings 15:1-3

*P*oor examples are like contagious diseases; so are talkative leaders who think mere terminology is all they need.

Eccles. 5:2

Woe unto the leader who is always right in his own sight, for he lives in the depth of deception and is dangerous to follow.

Prov. 14:12

A misled leader misleads his followers, resulting in double tragedy.

Matt. 15:14

When a leader is guided by blurred legal boundaries, he is liable to err; unless he sees his way clearly before proceeding, he is not safe to follow.

Matt. 15:14-15

The leader who allows his position to ruin him will often ruin many of his followers.

Prov. 16:18

It is safe to resign to God's dealings as well as his leadings. Leaders ought to know that first and foremost.

Ps. 119:67

A prospective leader must have challenges to propel him forward.

Exod. 3:1-10

Unless a leader is challenged daily to move beyond where he is he will never make progress to reach his ultimate goal.

Phil. 3:14

Unless a leader accepts the challenges which confront him daily, he will not be changing or be on his way to greater progress and usefulness.

2 Tim. 2:3-6

One of the greatest challenges in the life of a leader is the continual responsibility of making decisions of all kinds; some are more serious than others and have, therefore, more serious consequences.

Deut. 30:19-20

When a leader does not realize that God uses means, ways, and people on a daily basis to process us, he usually resists them and thus aborts God's process of maturity.

Rom. 8:28-29

A leader who seeks to have a life of sunshine without clouds will find he has no showers of blessing.

Ps. 23:4-5

The leader who shuns adversity keeps his best talents latent within him.

Mal. 3:3

The leader who is allowed to do absolutely what he pleases is basically a spoiled brat. Before long nothing will please him.

Eccles. 2:4-11

The measure of a leader is gauged by how he takes defeat and turns it into victory.

2 Cor. 4:7-11

10

No leader ever develops to his full potential without the continual addition of pressure and greater responsibilities.

Isa. 48:10

The leader who tackles difficulties that others shun discovers within himself hidden potential and abilities.

Matt. 25:14-30

The mightiest leader is the one who believes for success today, not tomorrow; his success today guarantees his success in the tomorrows to come.

2 Cor. 6:2

A leader who welcomes the tests of life objectively and diligently passes with high marks.

Ps. 105:19

Though a leader may learn some painful and costly lessons at times, these lessons can prove most beneficial in developing his leadership.

Job 23:10

A leader who goes through severe trials finds new meaning to the Scriptures applicable to his situation; he also finds God more real, near, and dear to him.

Phil. 2:5-8

Many times the Lord deems it necessary for a leader to be prepared for a new spiritual journey by a season of suffering, which he is often puzzled about until the Holy Spirit graciously quickens God's purposes to him.

1 Pet. 4:12-14

God works humility in His leaders in the face of false accusations that come from far and near as a part of the course called, "Leaders in the Making."

Ps. 27:12-14

An insecure leader is always deficient; he thinks everyone he faces is planning to attack him, and he categorizes everyone who differs with him as an opponent. No wonder he cannot find responsiveness in people, nor can he make a friend.

Rom. 8:31

Tested leaders are the ones who thrive on promotions; because they are realistic, they pass every test with flying colors.

Ps. 108:13

The leader who realizes the price of failure supercedes the price of success endeavors to obey God diligently without questioning, without hesitation, without reasoning, and without understanding, knowing this is God's secret of success.

1 Pet. 4:19

*O*bedience to God is the most costly thing in life. There is no use calculating the risks and the price; it is going to cost all.

Heb. 5:8-9

For a leader to be refined, he has to put himself totally in the hands of the Lord and welcome God's fire. What a price he has to pay. Yet that refinement will reflect the image of Christ in thought, word, and deed.

Mal. 3:1-3

The painful process that God takes a leader through is the price he pays for becoming what God has ordained him to be.

Heb. 12:3-11

There is no making of a leader without breaking first, and as long as God supervises all the ins and outs of his life, He produces a vessel fit for His use—but what a price.

2 Tim. 2:21

Whatever the price a leader has to pay in fulfilling the call of God upon his life, the dividends always exceed the cost.

1 Tim. 4:6-8

*A*s leaders, the price of helping others as leaders is being hurt by them at times for several reasons, for this is part of the role of leadership.

2 Cor. 12:15

The price of leadership includes accepting blame without justification, accepting criticism without retaliation, and accepting added pressure without resignation.

2 Cor. 6:1,3-10

An experienced leader knows that misunderstandings, misinterpretations, and misjudgments are bound to come; he knows the greatest price a man of God pays for serving God is to be misunderstood when he speaks the Word of the Lord. Therefore, he thoroughly prepares his heart for it.

John 15:18-20

Resentment against leadership is a part of the price leaders have to pay, regardless of the level of their position.

Num. 12:1-2

In His role of leadership, Jesus paid the price of laying down His life to reproduce after His own; so should everyone who is aspiring to a leadership role.

1 Pet. 2:21-23

The leader who pays the greatest price in preparation today is guaranteed the best leadership of tomorrow, because our effectiveness is related to our preparation.

Rev. 3:18-19

The leader who does not pay the price in know-how and self-discipline will never attain success.

2 Pet. 1:10

Wise leaders know that you cannot buy health in packages from either doctors, pharmacists, or health food stores, but health has to be gained and maintained at a great price that pays the greatest dividends.

3 John 2

Every leader deserves the best of health if he is willing to pay the best price and give his undivided attention to gain it.

1 Cor. 6:19-20

Also from Cityhill Publishing...

Called Out
A quarterly journal devoted to building the local church. $7.50 for a one-year subscription (four issues).

Living God's Way by Arthur Wallis
Nourishment for new believers. Mature Christians can use this study course to help newcomers get off to a strong start. $4.95

On To Maturity by Arthur Wallis
The next step for Christians who want to maintain their spiritual momentum. An insightful, practical, and challenging study course. $4.95

The Radical Christian by Arthur Wallis
A tough message, especially for those who prefer the status quo. A call to step beyond the safe limits of traditional religion. $5.95

China Miracle by Arthur Wallis
Americans whine about the cost of living. Chinese Christians count the cost of dying. Presents a pattern for revival in the West. $5.95

Available at your local Christian bookstore or direct from:
**Cityhill Publishing, 4600 Christian Fellowship Road
Columbia, MO 65203**
Please enclose payment and $1 for shipping with all orders.